Never split the right dice

Divide the dice wisely to optimize your strategic advantage

Lawrence S. Perkins

Copyright © 2023 by Lawrence S. Perkins

All rights reserved. No part of this publication may be reproduced, distributed, or transmitted in any form or by any means, including photocopying, recording, or other electronic or mechanical methods, without the prior written permission of the publisher, except in the case of brief quotations embodied in critical reviews and certain other noncommercial uses permitted by copyright law.

Table of contents

Introduction

One person with an interesting talent lived in a town surrounded by old trees and rolling hills: they could never split the right dice. This individual was a local mystery who had a strange knack for rolling dice in ways that were not expected.

When they rolled the dice in the bars or at get-togethers, this man's results were never predictable. When a high number was needed to win, the dice produced the lowest possible count. Similarly, there were times when a low roll was anticipated, but the dice unexpectedly rolled high.

The town was rocked by word of this abnormality spreading like wildfire. While some perceived it as a magical boon, others speculated that it might be a divine curse.

Academics traveled from far-off places to see this amazing dice-rolling event. They conjectured that there might be prophecies or old messages concealed inside these erratically rolled objects.

An extraordinary incident occurred one fatal evening, amid much anticipation and intellectual investigation. The dice One person with an interesting talent lived in a town surrounded by old trees and rolling hills: they could never split the right dice. This individual was a local mystery who had a strange knack for rolling dice in ways that were not expected.

When they rolled the dice in the bars or at get-togethers, this man's results were never predictable. When a high number was needed to win, the dice produced the lowest possible count. Similarly, there were times when a low roll was anticipated, but the dice unexpectedly rolled high.

The town was rocked by word of this abnormality spreading like wildfire. While some perceived it as a magical boon, others speculated that it might be a divine curse.

Academics traveled from far-off places to see this amazing dice-rolling event. They conjectured that there might be prophecies or old messages concealed inside these erratically rolled objects.

An extraordinary incident occurred one fatal evening, amid much anticipation and intellectual investigation. The dice rolled perfectly, matching the winning numbers every time. Disbelieving gasps flooded the crowd as it became silence.

After the initial shock subsided, it was clear that this unusual ability wasn't a sign of mystical abilities or fate. Rather, reflected a subliminal yearning for surprise and variation, an intrinsic yearning for life's unpredictable nature.

This person became a symbol—an embodiment of accepting life's unexpected journey—from that point on. Their dice turned into a treasured symbol, a prompt to enjoy life's unexpected dance and to treasure its turns and twists.
rolled perfectly, matching the winning numbers every time. Disbelieving gasps flooded the crowd as it became silent.

After the initial shock subsided, it was clear that this unusual ability wasn't a sign of mystical abilities or fate. Rather, it reflected a subliminal yearning for surprise and variation, an intrinsic yearning for life's unpredictable nature.

This person became a symbol—an embodiment of accepting life's unexpected journey—from that point on. Their dice turned into a treasured symbol, a prompt to enjoy life's unexpected dance and to treasure its turns and twists.

Never Split the Right Dice" is a tribute to the inventiveness of board games, painstakingly created by a group of dedicated creators. With its complex weave of strategy, luck, and wit, this engrossing game transports players to an immersive world where strategic decisions and dice rolls rule.

"Never Split the Right Dice" is essentially a game where players must navigate a landscape where each move has the potential to result in victory or defeat. The game encourages players to make wise decisions by balancing risks and rewards and accepting that dice rolling is erratic. With so many options available to them every turn, players must use cunning strategies to outwit their rivals and win.

This game is unique because it combines a well-thought-out strategy with the excitement of random events. The suspense grows with every dice roll as players plan and modify their strategy as needed. No two sessions are the same because of the dynamic gameplay that is always changing and thrilling.

With its carefully thought-out mechanics and elaborately constructed board, "Never Split the Right Dice" offers an immersive experience that will appeal to players of all skill levels. Players are encouraged to take advantage of opportunities, outwit rivals, or embrace the unpredictable nature of the game to go on an amazing trip full of surprises and the exhilaration of winning.

In the thrilling world of "Never Split the Right Dice," where every roll matters and every choice you make determines how you will win, accept mthe challenge, put your strategies to the test, and enjoy the thrill

Chapter1:Understanding the Game

Nestled among old forests and rolling hills in a charming community, there was a curious annual competition known as "Never Split the Right Dice." This highly regarded occasion was more than just a game; it was a test of cunning, good luck, and—above all—understanding.

The game was created long ago by the knowledgeable elders of the village to impart a basic understanding of strategy, teamwork, and the importance of understanding others. Every year when autumn's hues adorned the town, the residents gathered in the bustling central square, their hearts full of excitement for the spectacle that was about to take place.

A superb, intricately carved set of wooden dice, created by talented local artisans, was the centerpiece of this highly respected game.

There was an intellectual competition between two teams, each representing a different part of the town. Their task is to roll the dice, determine the numbers that appear, and then work together to come up with a plan that will allow them to get the most points without splitting the dice.

These mysterious dice held ethereal symbols that stood for various aspects of life, such as cooperation, empathy, unity, and trust. Stories and legends hinted at terrible outcomes if the correct dice were split, but the precise causes were still unknown.

There was excitement in the air as the game started. Teammates gathered close together, sharing ideas and discussing tactics as they cautiously glanced at the mysterious wooden cube. Some took a devious approach to the work, determined to maximize their points, while others were wary of the consequences of splitting the appropriate dice.

In the middle of the heated conversations and passionate arguments, two people stood out as symbols of comprehension. One was known for her sharp intuition and her constant sensitivity, and she felt that cooperation was important. The other, known for his extraordinary strategic acumen and foresight, saw the value of appreciating the goals and needs of every team member.

At a pivotal juncture, when the dice fell and settled, the numbers that emerged presented an enticing conundrum: a chance to score big points, but also a chance to divide the proper dice.

The atmosphere was tense. Disagreements erupted among the groups, with mayhem appearing to follow. From across the busy square, the two figures met eyes in the middle of this chaos. There was a mutual understanding between them in that silent exchange that went beyond words. They nodded subtly to lead their teams toward a compromise, a tactic that would maximize points without running the risk of a decisive split.

Their strategy combined empathy with intelligence, compassion, and insight. Once separated by competition and desire, both teams came together around a common goal. As their coordinated plan worked, applause broke out, not only for their success but also for the important lesson they had learned. The real winner of the game was not how many points were scored, but rather how the villagers accepted their newfound knowledge. These two people had demonstrated the value of listening, showing empathy, and working together to achieve a common objective. Their deeds had a far-reaching effect on the town's collective psyche for many generations to come. They instilled a culture of cooperation and collaboration that went beyond the yearly game.

Rules and Regulations

Never Split the Right" presents a unique viewpoint on bargaining tactics. Instead of focusing on dice or gaming laws, it takes inspiration from the experiences of a person with a history in high-stakes negotiations. Avoiding the widespread inclination to split things evenly to reach a compromise is the fundamental idea. Instead, it promotes a more sophisticated strategy that places a focus on understanding the viewpoint of the other side, active listening, and empathy.

This negotiation philosophy advises staying away from a win-lose perspective and focusing instead on finding solutions that satisfy the fundamental requirements and objectives of every party. It is suggested that strategies such as naming"Never Split the Right" presents a unique viewpoint on bargaining tactics. Instead of focusing on dice or gaming laws, it takes inspiration from the experiences of a person with a history in high-stakes negotiations. Avoiding the widespread inclination to split things evenly in order to reach a compromise is the fundamental idea. Instead, it promotes a more sophisticated strategy that places a focus on understanding the viewpoint of the other side, active listening, and empathy.

This negotiation philosophy advises staying away from a win-lose perspective and focusing instead on finding solutions that satisfy the fundamental requirements and objectives of each and every party. It [8] or dice-related laws and regulations. It seeks to assist people in navigating negotiations skillfully and pursuing mutually good outcomes by encouraging a more deliberate, sympathetic, and strategic approach.

emotions, asking thoughtful questions, asking tactical empathy, and mirroring be used to promote communication, reveal hidden details, and come to mutually beneficial agreements.

The book's ideas promote a reexamination of conventional negotiation tactics, even though its main focus isn't on games or dice-related laws and regulations. It seeks to assist people in navigating negotiations skillfully and pursuing mutually good outcomes by encouraging a more deliberate, sympathetic, and strategic approach

Strategies for Success

Deep Understanding: Use your in-depth knowledge of the game mechanics to inform your strategy and decision-making.

Player Dynamics: Adjust your game plan based on what your opponents are doing and how they are doing it.

Weigh the pros and drawbacks of every move to strengthen your position and strive for well-considered decisions. We call this kind of decision-making "balanced."

Tactical Negotiation: Develop your capacity for persuasion and willingness to make concessions in order to sway outcomes in your favor during negotiations.

Flexibility in Approach: Be adaptable and change your plan of action as the game and your opponents' actions change.

Opportunities for Collaboration: Seek out partnerships when they make sense, but exercise caution and good judgment when making decisions.

Resource Management: Optimize your in-game resources to increase their impact on your strategy as a whole.

Chapter 2:Choosing the Right Dice

Nestled among rolling hills and meandering rivers is the vibrant town of Ludoria, where a community of dedicated gamers gathered together. Their leader was a well-liked mentor whose skills were just as valuable as the sports they engaged in. In Ludoria, where laughter rang out from every alleyway and the thrill of the game infused every facet of everyday life, the throw of the dice held unparalleled significance. It often determined the outcome of major competitions and created bonds amongst rivals.

The annual gaming tournament in Ludoria was approaching, and excitement was in the air. Both seasoned players and novices honed their strategies, refined their skills, and picked out their dice with care, understanding that success hinged not only on cube selection but also on strategy.

As the day of the event drew near, there was a feeling of expectation. The mentor stood in front of the eager competitors, representing the wisdom of ganes and lending weight to their voice with experience and fairness. "Hello players," they greeted everyone, "choice of dice is important in our gaming universe. It has the key to both justice and excitement. To ensure a fair game, always remember that precision, superior materials, and firm adherence to the principle "Never Split the Right Dice" are essential.

The mentor guided the participants through the magical marketplace of Ludoria, which was populated with dice in every conceivable shape, color, and material. Along the way, the mentor discussed the significance of using premium materials to ensure the durability and fairness of each roll.

"Every die has its unique equilibrium, a dexterity that shapes a voyage through fate," they stated. Success depends more on talent, strategy, and the fairness of the dice than it does on luck."

The mentor used the glittering arrays of dice to highlight readability, size, and shape. Clear rolls were encouraged and misunderstanding was prevented during the competitive bouts with the use of standardized sizes and distinguishing markings.

"Remember," the instructor said, "different games require various dice." Each dice set, whether it's a polyhedral set for daring adventures or a standard six-sided cube for classic games, holds the spirit of its realm and should be chosen carefully."

As the game went on, players engaged in exciting battles where their fates were determined by the numbers on these everyday objects and each player had their own set of dice. Thanks to the guidance of the mentor and adherence to the principle of "Never Split the Right Dice," fairness triumphed during the competition.

The results of their dice rolls decided the fortunes of the two finalists who faced off in a thrilling final. The air crackled with suspense as the dice danced across the tables, each clattering out a fate. Because justice was served, the conclusion was both exhilarating and objective.

Ludoria was ablaze with cheers as the competition drew to a close, commemorating not just the winners but also the principles of fair play. The instructor smiled, realizing that the participants had had thrilling games and also maintained the spirit of justice in their gaming community by rolling the right dice and abiding by the game.

As a result, just as in real life, justice, integrity, and wise decision-making changed fate and produced amazing adventures in video games. The custom of correctly rolling the dice and abiding by the adage "Never Split the Right Dice" was deeply ingrained in Ludoria culture.

Types of Dice

In the vibrant realm of Polyhedralia, a diverse assortment of dice flourished; each had its own shape, purpose, and allure. At the heart of this vibrant world was the Dice Council, which had the following notable members: the well-known d20, the trustworthy d12, the upbeat d6, the adaptable d8, the precise d10, the enigmatic d4, and the elusive d100.

These dice were crucial to the evolving tales of the realm because of their elaborate designs and wide range of numbers. With its twenty-sided powers, the d20 was a master storyteller who captivated everyone with intricate tales of bravery and discovery.

Accompanying the d20 in combat, the dependable d12 emerged as a shield, skillfully rolling damage dice with a steady hand and consistent count, inspiring trust in everyone who sought its counsel.

The ubiquitous d6, with its bright and simple design, appeared in a significant number of games and charmed players worldwide with its straightforward familiarity and reliability.

Conversely, the d8, with its face having eight sides, stood for flexibility. Its unpredictable nature added excitement and intrigue to each roll and influenced the outcomes of many choices.

The precise and methodical d10 offered a variety of choices through percentile rolls; its accuracy served as a ray of hope in the face of chance and uncertainty.

The enigmatic d4, with its pointed pyramid form, enthralled players with its limited yet potent range, giving games unexpected turns and twists.

Last but not least, at the most pivotal moments in the history of gaming, the mysterious d100, a rare but significant sight, presided over percentile rolls, revealing intricate and subtle results.

Despite their diversity, the Polyhedralia dice recognized the power of unity. Taken as a whole, they embodied the finest aspects of luck and uncertainty, molding plots and drawing players into the captivating stories centered around the realm's gaming tables.

IMPORTANCE OF DICE

An unexpected revelation occurred as the negotiation moved forward under the guidance of the dice: the elders started to see patterns within the chaos. They understood that although the dice appeared random, they reflected the core of their group's knowledge. The way the numbers rolled seemed to connect with the complex subtleties of their conversations, gently nudging them in the direction of compromises that uphold tradition while welcoming innovation.

The dice came to represent harmony and justice. The results weren't only determined by chance; rather, it was a tool that represented the village's collective consciousness. Their dedication to cooperative decision-making was strengthened by this insight, which increased their level of faith in the procedure.

Furthermore, the peasants were impacted by the usage of dice. The younger generation was motivated to get more involved in village affairs by it. Early on in village gatherings, children were invited to participate in a reduced version of the dice bargaining, which helped them learn the ideals of cooperation and mutual understanding.

Villages nearby eventually learned about this creative approach to negotiation. Visitors inquiring to see this novel approach up close paid a visit. The use of dice as a bargaining tool started to expand across communities through exchange programs and shared experiences, promoting an inclusive decision-making and peaceful cohabitation culture.

The hitherto remote community rose to prominence as a hub for collaboration and progressive ideas. Once merely a collection of carved symbols, the dice have evolved into a respected relic, a sign of unanimity, and an example of how accepting ambiguity may lead to accord.

The driving force behind this revolutionary strategy, rose to prominence as a symbol of inspiring leadership. Her creativity not only transformed the village's bargaining process but also ignited a movement that brought communities from all over the world together to pursue just and equitable decision-making.

The dice's legacy persisted, acting as a timeless reminder that despite life's unpredictability, there is always room for harmony, comprehension, and a common goal of building a better tomorrow.

Chapter 3:Mastering Techniques

Within the field of technique mastery, there is a mysterious rule similar to the backgammon game's "Never split the right dice". This idea goes beyond the confines of any one discipline to symbolize the complex process of becoming proficient without having a name.

This mysterious concept at its root is the essence of deliberate refining. Just as the expression suggests grouping resources in the game, mastering techniques is about the art of refining talents with focus and accuracy as opposed to sprinkling efforts all over the place.

The significance of depth over breadth is emphasized by this nameless principle. True mastery arises from a thorough comprehension of a few fundamental concepts rather than from just touching the surface of numerous techniques. It echoes the idea of building on one's strengths rather than distributing them to strengthen one's competence.

This unidentified principle also has the wisdom to accept failure as a growth-promoting spark. Mastering tactics means being willing to make mistakes, learn from them, and keep improving, just as unlocking the phrase's secret meaning calls for perseverance and experience.

This idea also accepts the dichotomy of flexibility and structure. It recognizes the necessity for flexibility and supports an organized method for technique mastery, leaving freedom for creativity and adaptation within the bounds of accepted principles.

Finally, this nameless principle resonates with the quest for greatness across a wide range of disciplines and is independent of any specific field. Its enigmatic quality captures the spirit of mastery—a path devoid of a single term but marked by commitment, improvement, fortitude, and an unwavering search for a deeper comprehension.

Throwing Techniques

One day, in a city full of skyscrapers, teeming with the energy of ambitious negotiators, an enigmatic game—whose name has been forgotten with time—rose. The core of bargaining strategies is included within this game, which is played with specially designed dice.

An underlying knowledge of the significance of the game brought together a group of expert negotiators within this anonymous game. Under the guidance of a wise instructor known only as "The Guide," this secret organization explored the nuances of psychology, strategy, and the art of persuasion that are hidden behind every dice throw.

One of them was a skilled negotiator who could only be identified by their unparalleled skill at the game. Their talent was a masterful fusion of adaptation, intuition, and a hint of audacious unpredictability.

Another character, only known as "The Veteran," hovered in the shadows, an experienced negotiator whose reputation was clouded in mystery. Their methodical approach was characterized by well-considered throws that demonstrated their strategic knowledge and expertise.

Meetings of the society were private events where rumors of plans mixed with the sound of playing cards. The namelessness of the game itself served as a metaphor for the mystery and secrecy surrounding it.

But as rumors began to circulate and myths began to take hold, a competing group under the command of an intriguing figure known only as "The Challenger" surfaced from the murky depths of the negotiating underworld.

Shrouded in secrecy, their group aggressively challenged norms and customs.

A fight of cunning and strategy disguised as an unnamed game loomed on the horizon, marking the impending confrontation between these forces. As the dice began to fly, each roll serving as a calculated gambit in the covert war for domination, the tension in the air crackled.

The skilled negotiator made a move that left both sides reeling at a critical juncture, as the game was about to reach its peak. It was an unusual combination of chutzpah and intuition. With a calculated look on their face, the Veteran repositioned, taking advantage of the sudden change in direction.

The secret chamber resonated with the game's crescendo, casting shadows that swirled with suspense. Fortunately, the surprise move caused the Challenger's group to stumble, giving the society a well-deserved win.

The mythology of the nameless game expanded when the dust settled, surpassing its nondescript beginnings. Under the direction of The Guide, the community considered the lessons discovered—lessons that went beyond the boundaries of the game itself.

Ultimately, the unnamed game never was given, but its influence was woven into the legend of negotiation—a monument to the covert world of strategy, flexibility, and the tacit expertise of those who maneuvered through the murky waters of high-stakes talks.

Analyzing Opponents

Within the genre of strategy games, the captivating competition "Never Split the Right Dice" was the main attraction. Two formidable players surfaced in this dice and strategy game, their identities hidden in the competitive anonymity.

One player, a shrewd strategist, preferred bold moves, taking chances to frighten opponents and gain an early advantage. Their strategy was characterized by a daring that frequently caught opponents off guard and confused about what to do next.

The other, a mysterious wizard, cherished time and deliberate accuracy. Their approach was gradual and cloaked in an air of uncertainty that left opponents wondering. Their movements were calculated, every choice demonstrating a mind that had carefully considered every angle of the match.

Their battles were rumored to have been legendary among gamers. The way the plans interacted and the psychological battle that broke out with every dice roll astounded the spectators. Their silent duel became one of feints, bluffs, and subtle gestures.

The stress increased as the competition went on, and every roll had a match-ending consequence. The spectators were enthralled with the intensity of the match, seeing an impressive demonstration of strategy and forethought.

There was a buzz of excitement in the air during the final confrontation. With precision, the players completed their last rolls, bringing their disparate strategies together in a stunning demonstration of skill and intelligence. One player pursued a strategy of high risk, and high reward, and without dividing, he or she achieved an astounding sum. The other, playing more calmly and methodically, managed to score just as well without risking their dice.

Their match served as a testament to the difficulties in assessing opponents in a game where the suspense was increased by anonymity. It was a fascinating spectacle, a wordless struggle in which the only things that counted were the mastery of strategy and the intelligence of two supremely intelligent people competing in the ultimate game of wits.

Chapter 4:Advanced Strategies

The yearly competition known as "Never Split the Right Dice" was the most prestigious challenge in the lively kingdom of Ludoria, where games were praised as intelligence and strategic tests. There were rumors that this game was brought to the kingdom by mysterious Dice Gods, drawing the most daring brains from all over.

Amidst this joyous occasion, a mysterious participant materialized—a person whose identity was concealed behind a mask of anonymity. This player, a master of unconventional strategy, faced off against a strong opponent in the competition and was prepared to reveal a plan of attack that broke all rules.

The game started with the sound of dice clattering through the hallway. The first roll came up with a modest total, but the anonymous player decided to try something different and kept one die while rolling over the other. As this unorthodox choice came to pass, gasps resounded.

The gamer consistently produced captivating displays of strategic skill, never once splitting the right die. Every play appeared nonsensical, yet it paved the way for victory, gradually building up an incredible total that baffled the opponent and spectators alike.

The opponent, a seasoned veteran renowned for their tactical acumen, found it difficult to understand this unconventional strategy. They tried to counter but instead became caught in the maze of the player's unorthodox approach.

When the game was about to reach its peak, the enigmatic player made one last roll and revealed a combination that guaranteed the highest possible total without ever going against the split-the-right die rule. As the player declared victory, the crowd erupted in deafening acclaim, making a lasting impression on the history of the game.

The story of this bold move reverberated throughout Ludoria, igniting players' passion and inquisitiveness to venture into hitherto undiscovered territories in "Never Split the Right Dice." The enigmatic winner's legacy persisted as evidence of the unrelenting inventiveness and inventiveness that transformed the terrain of this cherished game.

Risk Management

A strange game known as "Fate's Dance" captivated players in the world of Shadowsong with the seduction of chance and danger. The center of this captivating competition was an ancient bar called the "Twilight Hearth," which was tucked away among the cobblestone streets of the historic city.

A mysterious pair of dice made by expert craftsmen from a bygone era was at the center of Fate's Dance. The Left and Right dice were more than simply tools; they were doors to uncharted territory, with the potential for both the glory of victory and the heartbreak of defeat.

A diverse group of gamers, each representing a unique approach to risk management, gathered around the softly illuminated tables of the Twilight Hearth. There was the Bold Bard, whose soul jived with the erratic possibilities of the Right die, spinning tales of audacious exploits and exhilarating triumphs. The astute alchemist sat across from the bard, methodically formulating plans, playing the game sensibly, and favoring the stability of the left dice.

Anticipation crackled in the air like static as the game unfolded amid the quiet atmosphere of the tavern. The sound of dice clattering on wooden tables was interspersed with cheers and gasps. Fate swung pendulously, throwing equal parts misfortune and prosperity into shadows.

The Bold Bard's acrobatics reached thrilling new heights, evoking gasps and cheers from bystanders while occasionally plunging into the unknown. On the other side of the poet, the astute alchemist's well-thought-out moves ensured steady advancement, protected from the random fluctuations of fate.

In the midst of these disparate players, an enigmatic outsider, concealed by a hooded cloak, prowled the edges of the game. Even the most intelligent spectators were puzzled by this mysterious figure's unanticipated elegance as she performed with an air of ambiguity.

The game came to a close as nightfall settled over the tavern, creating a tapestry of shadows and flickering lighting. Unexpectedly, neither the bold gambits of the adventurous bard nor the cautious plans of the astute alchemist proved to be successful. Rather, the enigmatic nomad, shrouded in secrecy, declared victory, their unconventional approach to risk management surpassing norms and expectations.

Rumors began to circulate throughout the tavern, tales of the mysterious "Fate's Dance" that transcended style and approach, lingering in the shadows like an enigma waiting for the inquisitive minds that dared to participate in its alluring waltz, spread like wildfire. The tales taught about the art of risk management.

Reading Patterns and Tells

An expert negotiator refined their craft in analyzing patterns and tells inside high-stakes agreements in a city buzzing with possibility and intrigue. Their notoriety preceded them, rumored in dark corners and sought after by those looking for their knowledge.

One day, an intriguing invitation arrived, a summons to an unannounced meeting from an unidentified sender going only by the handle "The Enigma." Attracted by the attraction of secrecy, the negotiator accepted the offer and went off to a secret place outside of town.

The negotiator stepped inside a dark, magnificent room and saw a figure shrouded in mystery. The mysterious host, faceless, held up an old book with mysterious symbols scratched all over its pages. This ancient book promised to provide the most profound techniques for negotiating—the nuanced craft of identifying patterns and revealing clues concealed in the complex dance of exchanges.

Examining the obscure manuscript with no names or traditional lessons, the mediator discovered some very important information. The manuscript, devoid of names or precise references, revealed novel strategies to decipher nonverbal signs and maneuver through even the most complex conversations, challenging the fundamental assumptions of negotiation theory.

Over time, the negotiator assimilated the information contained in the mysterious text, revealing a previously unheard-of comprehension of human behavior during talks. Their talents increased with every page that was decoded, enabling them to see and decipher subtle signs that were outside the typical realm.

Equipped with this acquired knowledge, the negotiator skillfully handled complex negotiations, revealing hidden agendas and accurately interpreting complex cues. As word got out about their extraordinary ability to uncover their opponents' hidden agendas, their reputation grew.

But this enhanced authority also meant a moral cost. The negotiator struggled with the moral conundrum of using such sway in talks. They debated the thin line that separates using one's abilities for one's own benefit from using them for the benefit of society as a whole.

After giving it some thought, the negotiator decided on something firm. Instead of using their unparalleled negotiating skills to manipulate others, they would use them to forge fair agreements, build coalitions, settle disputes, and create chances that would benefit all sides equally.

As a result, the negotiator became known not only as an expert at seeing patterns and cues but also as a symbol of justice and integrity—an nameless enigma who led talks toward balance and harmony in the complex web of human connection.

Chapter 5:Avoiding Common Mistakes

There once was a young wizard who, in a world cloaked in ambiguity and illuminated by magical powers, followed his voracious curiosity to the center of perplexing riddles. He heard murmurs of a long-forgotten game called "Untamed Arcane."

The core of the game was revealed when he discovered an old manuscript covered in mysterious symbols deep within the old library of an unknown city. It alerted us to a dangerous error: breaking the Arcane Core.

The document warned of dire consequences for anybody who dared give in to this temptation, stating that doing so would upset the delicate balance of the world's magical essence and unleash immense chaos.

Fueled by a desire to learn more and comprehend this mysterious occult mystery, the mage set out on a mission. He traveled across magical countries, from busy cities to peaceful meadows, in search of the counsel of sages and the direction of hermits living in seclusion.

At the end of his journey, on top of an unnamed peak covered in mist, he came across a sage whose eyes gleamed with age-old wisdom. The sage disclosed the secret of the game: although the Arcane Core has great power, breaking it may throw the realm into chaos.

Under the guidance of the sage, the magician explored the depths of "Untamed Arcane," learning how to harness its power without giving in to the need to shatter the Arcane Core. As he refined his abilities and internalized the sage's lessons, time turned into his ally.

With a renewed sense of understanding and an unwavering determination, the wizard went back to the city that was not called, where "Untamed Arcane" competitions were taking place. Proficient adversaries frequently succumbed to the temptation of dividing the Arcane Core, enticed by instant benefits.

Nevertheless, the mage performed with exactitude, demonstrating proficiency and eschewing the fatal mistake forewarned by the old manuscript. His every action demonstrated his strategic skill and guaranteed that the magical equilibrium of the realm would not be upset.

His victories told stories of wisdom and moderation that reverberated throughout the unnamed nations. The mage's legacy was transformed into a warning story, illustrating the perils of temptation and the triumph of wisdom over carelessness. So the world flourished under the protection of a mage who maintained the Arcane Core's oneness and kept the magical energies wild but entire.

Pitfalls to Dodge

Scene 1: The Battle in the Boardroom

Determined to obtain a strategic alliance for her company, a determined executive prepares for a critical negotiation in a sleek corporate tower with a possible business partner. Motivated by the idea of "Never Split the Difference," she gets ready carefully and has a customized plan to seal the purchase.

Scene 2: The Trap of Rigidity

When the discussions start, the CEO insists that a fixed pricing structure is the best course of action and forcefully anchors the conversation around it. The prospective partner, however, indicates interest in looking at more expansive parameters that include timeframe commitments and service delivery. She changes her approach and emphasizes the company's flexibility and dedication to providing specialized services after realizing that her rigidity may endanger the discussions.

Scene 3: The Mirage of Emotion

The executive talks about service levels and then dives into statistical analysis, ignoring the partner's subtly expressed reservations about the company's delivery schedule for a moment. When she senses hesitancy, she shifts into sympathetic listening. Recognizing the issues, she offers an updated service plan that meets expectations and restores the emotional bond that is necessary for advancement.

Scene 4: The Ready Turnaround

The executive was taken aback when the partner abruptly voiced reservations regarding the company's intention to expand into new regions. Her careful planning, though, comes through. She quickly turns the conversation in her favor by incorporating insights from market research into her pitch, highlighting the company's thorough expansion strategy and allaying concerns.

Scene 5: The Horizon Beyond the Deal

After focusing mostly on cost and services, the CEO discovers that the partner is also considering possible long-term partnerships that go beyond the current transaction. By changing her strategy, she increases the scope of the discussion by showcasing the business's creative potential for joint ventures and future growth prospects.

Scene 6: The Junction of Clarification

The executive momentarily believes that the partner's main priority is cost containment. But she stops to ask for further information. This indicates that creating a solid, win-win alliance is the partner's top objective. The executive quickly adjusts her focus so that her suggestion is in line with the partner's strategic plan.

Scene 7: A Win-Win Resolution as the Finale

When the discussions come to an end, the executive's ability to remain composed under duress is crucial. She pays attention to the partner's nonverbal clues and actively listens, which results in a reworked proposal that meets needs and closes a lucrative agreement for her business. They exchange smiles and a handshake to complete the deal, laying the groundwork for a fruitful collaboration.

In summary, the CEO successfully navigates the negotiation minefield by skillfully avoiding obstacles with emotional intelligence, adaptability, careful planning, a comprehensive value proposal, patience, and active listening. The image fades as she leaves, assured that she has not only struck a bargain but also laid the groundwork for a fruitful and profitable partnership.

Learning from Errors

A gang of daring explorers set out on a mission to discover the mysteries of a mysterious board game known only as "The Enchanted Dice," where old tales whispered. These people, whose identities have been lost to time, had special abilities and unflinching resolve.

They entered the magical and mysterious world of the Enchanted Dice, guided by ancient scrolls and mysterious maps. The adventurers had to make difficult choices when the dice rolled, revealing numbers that would determine their fate: add, subtract, multiply, or divide.

They had a cunning and resourceful commander who skillfully handled the intricacies of the game. But even this mysterious boss made mistakes from time to time. A crucial error in judgment sent them in the wrong direction, putting doubt on their search for the game's elusive prizes.

Instead of giving up and becoming hopeless, the group came together and accepted the idea that mistakes were chances for improvement rather than setbacks. They became fully engrossed in the complexities of the game, developing their abilities and coming up with creative solutions to overcome the obstacles that were ahead.

A player with an aptitude for deciphering clues among the explorers found buried clues in the game's design. These mysterious cues revealed techniques to decipher the actual meaning of the Enchanted Dice.

Another, quick-witted and agile, projected possible results and quickly adjusted to unanticipated events. Their fast thinking frequently turned setbacks into unanticipated victories.

They encountered obstacles along the way that put their fortitude, guile, and togetherness to the test as they traveled through magical settings. With every task, participants learned more about the core of the game and themselves, discovering deep truths that were reflected in the decisions they took.

Their showdown was ahead of them: a showdown with the mysterious creature hiding as the Dice Dragon, the game's guardian. The adventurers prevailed in a decisive fight that put their will to the test and unlocked the game's greatest treasure—a deep comprehension of the transformational potential of learning from failures.

After completing their journey, the explorers returned with strengthened friendships, newfound understanding, and a firm conviction that mistakes may be used as stepping stones to enlightenment. Their story vanished into the pages of history, a mythical illustration of the timeless truth that there is always room for improvement and enlightenment.

Chapter 6:Advanced Gameplay

In a world where games were mystical, there was a mysterious activity called the Challenge, which was a more complex version of the old game "Never Split the Right Dice." This mysterious challenge drew players from all around the world, who were all competing for mastery while remaining anonymous and battling for fame or recognition.

A unique individual, an unidentified strategist distinguished solely by their unmatched proficiency in the game's art, stood out among these anonymous participants. The gaming elite talked quietly about their prowess in figuring out the Challenge's intricacies.

This anonymous gamer set out on a solo quest, stumbling through the Challenge's maze-like twists and turns with an almost supernatural accuracy that defied explanation. Their movements were perfectly timed, foreseeing their opponents' plans and skillfully swaying the outcome in their favor.

The strategist without a name faced strong opponents throughout the Challenge, all of them eager to try their mettle against this elusive master. Time and again, however, the player who remained unknown won; their invisibility took on a sense of mystery that added to their attraction.

Within the gaming community, rumors were circulating regarding this mysterious player's genuine identity. Some conjectured that they were a solitary genius, while others thought they were a group of extraordinarily intelligent people coming together to overcome the Challenge.

In a dramatic showdown, the Challenge reached its pinnacle with greater stakes than previously. The contest that would decide who was the supreme game master pitted the unnamed strategist against a challenger whose abilities matched their own.

The final battle played out in a spectacle that had the gaming community in awe, with every move performed with the dexterity of a master. When the dice were rolled, symbols lined up in complex patterns that only the sharpest minds could figure out. The game hung precariously, and there was a tangible tension in the air.

The anonymous player produced an amazing show of cunning, arranging a series of movements that defied reason and confused even the most seasoned onlookers. They won the game by following the golden rule, which is to never split the right dice, and did it in a way that astounded spectators.

The anonymous strategist's identity remained a secret when the competition came to an end, but their legacy was inscribed in the

Challenge's annals. They disappeared into the night, leaving a legacy that was more than just recognizable; it was a monument to the unnamed genius of strategy and the unfathomable desire to become the best at the complex game of strategy.

Complex Scenarios

The finding of the Right Dice changed the path of history in a world rich in folklore. Divided across realities to avert calamitous occurrences, these relics have great power and might be dangerous if reunited.

In the midst of this, a brave person appeared and was praised for their bravery and intelligence. With the mission of protecting the broken dice pieces, this warrior traveled through dangerous environments and strange phenomena brought about by the broken dice's energy.

The effects of the dice's power became clear to them on their voyage. In one universe, the fractured power of the dice engulfed a town in permanent darkness, tormenting its residents with never-ending nightmares. The village was freed from the dice's evil hold by the hero's empathy and resourcefulness.

Time flowed wildly in another dimension, presenting a warped reality. Here, the protagonist had to deal with the unpredictable consequences of the dice fragment and use rapid thinking to piece together evidence that would eventually take him to the evil force behind the havoc.

The hero was about to face the evil force that was trying to put the dice back together. In a pivotal battle, the protagonist foiled the antagonist's schemes by restraining himself from fusing the pieces and instead employing their combined powers to neutralize the danger.

After giving the Right Dice back to its guardians, the hero took up the role of keeper of these relics and committed their entire life to learning the significance of the dice. They read old books and predictions and realized that if the pieces were put back together, it could be catastrophic.

Difficulties continued as groups formed, some calling for unity to bring about advancement and others clinging to the old prescription. The guardian balanced these divergent opinions, trying to maintain peace and avoid abusing the power of the dice.

In the end, communication and cooperation led to a compromise. The guardian suggested forming a council that brought together a variety of viewpoints, which resulted in policies that encouraged cooperation while upholding the decree. Under this sensible strategy, Eldoria prospered, welcoming innovation while upholding tradition.

The guardian's legacy persisted, instructing succeeding generations on how to responsibly examine the energies on the dice. An institute was founded to comprehend the artifacts, stressing the need to exercise prudence and discernment when delving into their mysteries.

Eldoria flourished over time, a monument to the fine balance between tradition and advancement, molded by the unshakable commitment and selfless deeds of the defender who made sure the Right Dice would always be a force for harmony rather than disarray.

Strategic Decision-Making

The Dice Tournament was a captivating event that drew competitors from throughout the realm of Arlanda. One of them was an enigmatic tactician whose identity was concealed behind a mask of anonymity. Their reputation as a mysterious player with unmatched cunning and strategic brilliance precedes them.

This strategist captured the attention of onlookers right from the start of the competition with their unique and compelling strategies. The spectators were enthralled as each match developed like an exciting narrative, with the strategist handling the dice with an almost supernatural dexterity. Their style of play was an elaborate ballet of planned risks and bold moves, akin to an art form.

The strategist faced a wide range of opponents as the event progressed through its rounds, each of whom offered a different challenge. While some opponents used a slow and methodical approach, others preferred aggressive splitting techniques. Every game turned into a platform for the strategist's creativity and adaptation.

The semi-finals got more intense as the strategist squared off against an unpredictable opponent. A calculated dance began, each step a calculated risk. When the time came, the strategist surprised their opponent by veering from their regular course and selecting an unexpected route that left their opponent speechless.

The last match pitted the strategist against the current champion, a respected veteran praised for their strategic brilliance. It was a battle of the Titans. A cerebral contest broke out, with every move matched by an equally fascinating countermove. When the game came down to a close, the strategist was faced with a crucial choice.

They bravely broke with tradition and set off on an improbable voyage, surpassing expectations. Their fate was sealed as the dice fell. The gamble was richly rewarded, giving the strategist a close but assured victory over the champion. The strategist prevailed, and the arena exploded in loud applause, leaving an enduring story of strategic genius etched in the annals of Arlandia's Dice Tournament.

Conclusion

There was an unusual antique shop tucked away between undulating hills in the center of a peaceful town. Treasures from bygone centuries adorned the shelves, each one speaking a tale of bygone days. A set of dice that were rumored to possess magical abilities was found among the other artifacts. It was said that these dice, if left intact, would never split unevenly, making every roll a perfect match.

A young person accidentally went into the charming store one day. Attracted by a mysterious force, the guest encountered the mysterious store owner, a guy only known as "Keeper." Keeper warned the newbie, "Never split the right dice," with a somewhat enigmatic smirk.

Unidentified and curious, the guest bought the dice and took them with him. They were giddy with anticipation as they rolled the dice, amazed at the perfect symmetry that appeared each time.

Weeks passed, and the anonymous spirit was unable to resist the constant urge to defy destiny. Disregarding Keeper's caution, they wondered what would happen if the dice divided.

The anonymous one threw the dice again, this time with a mixture of interest and trepidation. Something supernatural surged as the dice left their hand, sending a tremor through reality. The dice parted, and for a single second, everything seemed to stop.

The world changed in that moment. Time reversed, circumstances were rearranged, and the anonymous spirits discovered themselves in a changed world where each choice they made took them down unexpected and strange avenues.

The anonymous one, desperate to return to the peace of their previous existence, turned to Keeper for advice. Keeper spoke again, gently this time, "Never split the right dice," sympathy shining in his eyes. He clarified that manipulating the dice would upset the natural order because they contained the strands of destiny.

The nameless spirit took the weight of their deeds with a sorrowful heart. They accepted the new world, figuring out how to go through its curves and seeing beauty in the unexpected.

Over the next few days, the anonymous one found moments of happiness and insight in this other world and cherished what made it special. They continued, taking comfort in the commonplace and cherishing every moment that remained unchanged.

The dice stayed intact, a silent record of the voyage of the unnamed soul, a warning that some riddles were best left unanswered and that some pathways were meant to be followed exactly as written. And thus the legend—never split the right dice—persisted in the town's rumors and whispers.

www.ingramcontent.com/pod-product-compliance
Lightning Source LLC
Chambersburg PA
CBHW050049260726

48658CB00005B/1855